With best wishes,

Bernard Baldwin

# Mountain Ash
## and Penrhiwceiber
# Remembered
# in pictures

by

## Bernard Baldwin, M.B.E.

D. BROWN AND SONS
COWBRIDGE AND BRIDGEND
1986

ISBN 0 905928 50 4

# ACKNOWLEDGEMENTS

Many of the photographs in this volume have very kindly been lent by Mr. Les Price of Mountain Ash who has a propensity for discovering history in our midst—places, people, events—and some of his shots are magnificent. Les's scent for history also took him to the homes of retired people—Cliff Parfitt the shoemaker was one—and his shots of them are intimate and thought-provoking. He qualifies as a picture historian if nothing else.

I must also thank Messrs. Bernard Davies, Bill Smith, George Fry, Gwessin Jones, David Ingram, David Bethell, D. K. Jones, Bill Thomas, Bob Mansell, Conway Stuart, W. A. Loosemore, William Jex, David Sellick, Llew Miles, Bill Williams, Arthur Hillier, Father David Yeoman, Terry Llewellyn, G. Armstrong (Warsop), Vic Llewelyn, Tom Fantham, Ron Bevan, K. D. Williams, Ken Parry, W. G. Sweet, Dennis Davies, Bill Perkins, Edgar George, Ted Demery, Lord Aberdare, Mountain Ash Library, Y.M.C.A., and Rugby Football club, and the Aberdare Leader.

Many ladies helped too, either with the loan of photographs or by identifying people or places or events. I include Mrs. Doris Brooks, Miss Nancy and Miss Gladys Christopher, Miss Sheila Bennett, Mrs. D. Way, Mrs. P. Nelson, Mrs. M. E. Nelson, Mrs. Irene Weekes, Mrs. E. Rawlins, Mrs. Lydia Cameron, Mrs. E. Webber, Miss J. Thomas, Coun. Mrs. Mia George-Johnson, Mrs. Eunice Morgan, Mrs. Barbara Gibson, Mrs. Maisie Creech, Mrs. Thelma Bevan, Mrs. Vanessa Williams, Nurse Val Davies, Mrs. B. Broom, Mrs. H. Summerill, Mrs. M. Richards, Mrs. Hilda Francis, Mrs. M. Hayes, Mrs. Marion Jones, Mrs. Pauline Jarman, Mrs. E. G. Harding, Miss Nicola Suggett.

*Printed in Wales by D. Brown & Sons Ltd., Cowbridge and Bridgend, Glamorgan*

1  Lord Edmund-Davies of Aberpennar

*(Photograph by David Bethell)*

# Foreword

### *by Lord Edmund-Davies of Aberpennar*

Mr. Bernard Baldwin's last book *Mountain Ash Remembered* was praised and warmly welcomed by many 'Mount' folk. It reminded Cynon Valley men and women of all ages of a host of incidents (some happy and some sad, the naturally important as well as the purely local) which go to make up the chequered history of our birthplace.

Mr. Baldwin's new book will doubtless again be warmly welcomed as a fascinating pictorial presentation of aspects of that history. I feel sure that it will be appreciated by very many 'Mount' folk, and perhaps particularly by those of us who have for many years lived away from our birthplace but nevertheless still recall with affection and pride the Cynon Valley as we knew it so long ago.

I am certainly one of their number, and I am glad of this opportunity of saying so. I wish Mr. Baldwin and his new book good fortune.

*May 1986*

*Overleaf 2*   Her Majesty the Queen, then Princess Elizabeth, shortly after her investiture as Honorary Ovate of the Gorsedd of Bards of Wales, in Duffryn Woods, Mountain Ash on 6th August, 1946

# Royalty

3  Princess Elizabeth awaits the Bardic Ceremony at the National Eisteddfod, Mountain Ash, 1946

4  Princess Elizabeth at the Bardic Ceremony

H.R.H. Princess Elizabeth bein
invested as Honorary Ovate o
the Gorsedd of the Bards o
Wales at Mountain Ash
Glamorgan, 6th August, 194

**5** Princess Elizabeth takes the oath

**6**  The Princess chats informally to Lord Hall, Geoffrey S. Morgan and others in Gwernifor Grounds, 6th August, 1946

**7**  The Queen Mother, then Duchess of York, accompanied by Lord Hall of Cynon Valley and the Hon. John Bruce, is here pictured being presented to members of the Y.M.C.A. and British Legion outside the Y.M.C.A. Rooms in Pryce Street

# The Town and Surroundings

**8** Mountain Ash in 1850

**9** Mountain Ash in 1860

Caegarw and Bridge, Mountain Ash

10  Mountain Ash bridge and a view of Caegarw, 1899

11  Caegarw, 1920

Mountain Ash    East Side

A Joyous Christmas To You

General View,
Caegarw, Mountain Ash. 459.

**12** Ffrwd Crescent, St. Margaret's Church and a part of Caegarw, 1921

**13** Caegarw from Bryngolwg School, Miskin, 1921. The Pavilion can be seen in the middle of the left hand side

CAEGARW FROM THE CENTRAL SCHOOL

A View from the Mountain. Mountain Ash 762

14 A view of Miskin and Caegarw from Darran Las, 1922

15 A general view of the town, 1924

**16**  A general view of Penrhiwceiber, 1930s

**17**  The heart of Mountain Ash from the air, 1930s

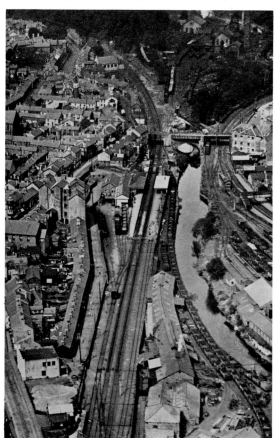

**18** A 1930s view of the General Hospital, Mountain Ash

**19** St. Mary's Church, Miskin, now Our Lady of Lourdes Church, with Darran Las in the background

**20** St. Margaret's Church in 1862

**21** A 1984 shot of St. Margaret's Church before the restoration work of the south wall began

**22** Inside St. Margaret's, 1984

**23**  Upper Oxford Street, *c.* 1900

**24**  Lower Oxford Street, *c.* 1904

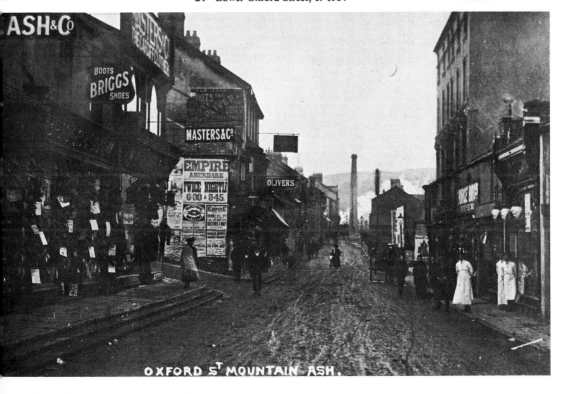

25 Lower Oxford Street, *c.* 1905

26 Upper Oxford Street, *c.* 1906

*Oxford Street, Mountain Ash*

27  Oxford Street, *c.* 1908

28  Oxford Street, *c.* 1920s

29  Oxford Street before vehicular traffic

30  Commercial Street, 1927

**31** The famous icecream cart of Rabaiotti's, in Phillip Street, 1907

**32** In Bailey Street, 1907. The handcart sold Evening Dresses on the street.

**33** The Cottage Hospital, Granville Terrace in 1908. The building later became the Maternity Home—now a block of flats

**34** Nixon's Workmen's Hall, 1920. The poster advertises Vint's Scenorama at the hall's Public Theatre. Vint was a well known impresario

**35**  Lower Penrhiwceiber Road, *c.* 1890

**36**  Upper Penrhiwceiber Road, *c.* 1890

**37** Workmen's hall, Penrhiwceiber Road, *c.* 1910

**38** Another shot of the Workmen's Hall, Penrhiwceiber Road, *c.* 1912

**39** *(left)* The front room of the home of Mr. & Mrs. Sidney Bond, Belgrade Villa, Woodfield Terrace, Penrhiwceiber, in 1920

**40** *(right)* Mountain Ash Town Hall and bridge, 1926

**41** Mountain Ash bridge and Darranlas from Ffrwd Crescent and bridge

**42** After the bomb. Only one bomb actually hit anything during the war. It was Duffryn School—at night when the school was empty. This 1940 shot shows the school after the bomb, with Caegarw in the background

**43** The "tin shanty", home of the first County (Grammar) School, 1912

COUNTY SCHOOLS, MOUNTAIN ASH.

**45** A modest flooding in Henry Street in 1960 shows P.C. Casey in the bow, Sergeant Edgar George centre and P.C. John Davies using a shovel for an oar after effecting a rescue

**44** A typical rescue scene in Henry Street each year

**47** Mountain Ash bridge, 6th December, 1960

**46** The tide mark shows the extent of the flooding at the Miskin Inn, in December, 1960

**48**  This was a familiar scene from Mountain Ash bridge each winter. The Cardiff Road and Oxford Street stations were flooded above platform level

**49**  This scene in Oxford Street shows Mr. Alec Cameron's yacht, Cameronia II negotiating the bend in the road from its Knight Street garage where it was built, in 1958. The Police Sergeant in the foreground is Sergeant 639 Islwyn Thomas. Mr. Ted Webber, who owned the garage where the yacht was built, is the man on the road to the right; Mr. Fred Jacob is the man nearby with the pipe. Mr. John Webber is the man looking back. Miss Gillian Phillips is the young lady behind Ted Webber, and behind her is Tommy ("Tosh") Thomas. On the left hand side opposite the cab of the lorry is Mr. Harry Pidgeon, in front of him is Mr. John Jones with the pipe, and the lady in the front left is Mrs. Ethel Evans (Ffrwd Chapel House)

# Groups and Personalities

**50** Mountain Ash Constitutional Club, winners of the A.C.C. All England Billiards Challenge Shield, 1902, and the South Wales A.C.C. Billiards Shield, 1901-2, 1902-3.
Standing, left to right: E. R. McGregor (capt.), T. P. Cole (marker).
Seated: Geo. Sellick, Geo. Williams

**51**  Penrhiwceiber Fire Brigade, 1908

**52**  Class One, Newtown Primary School, 1916

53  Newtown Juvenile Prize Choir, 1920. Winners of the National Eisteddfod in Neath in 1918, the South Wales Challenge Shield in 1917, -18, and -19, and the Great Welsh Musical Festival in 1920

54  Bryngolwg Church Soup Kitchen, Miskin, May, 1921

55  Gough's charabanc outing, 1919. Note the solid rubber tyres

56  A Model 'T' Ford, 1922, with driver Jack Bond and family aboard outside their Belgrade Villa, Woodfield Terrace, Penrhiwceiber home in 1923

**57** The great evangelist Gipsy Smith came to the Pavilion in 1909. Photo shows him seated centre front row, 6th from left, with a long flowing moustache

**58** Officers and brothers of the Royal Antediluvian Order of the Buffaloes, April, 1928

59　The five Clinch brothers, left to right: Michael, Edward, Thomas, Patrick and John. John was father of Mrs. Monica Hayes, of Fernhill

60　Winners of Mountain Ash Sub-Division Bowls Competition, 1931.
Back row, left to right: P.C. 709, D. George, Sgt. 526, A. H. Kirby, Sgt. 176, T. Clark (capt.),
P.C. 299, W. J. Thomas
Front row: Supt. E. Jones (President), Insp. J. Clinch, (Vice-President)

**61** Councillor John Christopher, Chairman of Mountain Ash Council, opens the New Cardiff Road in 1933

**62** A 1940 photograph of Mountain Ash St. John Ambulance Brigade.
Seated centre is Superintendent Mr. Bob Batty

**63** Darran Road Methodist Church Guild, 1942. The A.T.C. Cadet on the right is Fred Horler; seated front left is Aubrey Williams (buses). Seated centre are Pat Baldwin, Ivy Morris, Ethel Williams, Edna Anstee, Eileen Rivers and Elwyn Neate

**64** Terry Llewellyn, son of Dai, and his "Wild Ones", 1958

**65** A 1958 photo of the nurses and staff from the Merthyr and Aberdare Hospital Management Committee, following the passing-out examination of two years earlier. Among those present were Coun. Arthur Hillier, Matron Williams, Sister Morgan, Mr. Ivor Davies, (Hospital Management Sec.), Mrs. Elizabeth Christopher, Mrs. Margaret Truman-Thomas and Miss Lillian Mutter

**66** The parade on Civic Sunday to inaugurate Coun. Arthur Hillier as Chairman of Mountain Ash Council, May 1958

**67** Parade of the High Constable of Miskin Higher, 1968. High Constable Mr. John Morgan and Mrs. June Morgan lead the parade to St. Margaret's Church

**68** The Civic Parade through Oxford Street on the occasion of the inauguration of the first Mayor of Cynon Valley, Councillor William Morgan, in 1974

**69** The old manor house which stood on the site of the present Dyffryn House

**70** Coat of Arms of the Lord Aberdare family

**71** The Aberdare Family, 1900. Henry Austin Bruce, first Lord Aberdare, was married twice. By his first marriage he had three daughters and a son, of whom two, Margaret and Rachel are identified in the photograph. By his second marriage he had 7 daughters and 2 sons, of whom Caroline, Nora, Pamela, Alice, William and Charles are identified. Also in the photograph are the wives of William and Charles and the husbands of Margaret and Nora. Seated left to right: William Bruce, son; Emily, wife of William; Nora Whateley, daughter; Lord Aberdare; Finetta, wife of Charles; Lady Aberdare; Margaret Richmond, daughter. Standing left to right: Rachel, daughter; Henry Whateley, Alice Bruce, daughter; Pamela Bruce, daughter; Charles Bruce, son;

72  Henry Austin Bruce, the first Lord Aberdare—a picture taken by Robert Crawshay of Merthyr

73  Dyffryn House, now threatened with demolition

*Duffryn House, Mountain Ash*

**74** The two Gurkha soldiers who were servants at Dyffryn House

**75** One of the grand fireplaces in Dyffryn House

**76** *(left)* Dai Llewellyn in his famous pose as "Popeye the sailorman"

**77** *(right)* King George Vth invests Sergeant Robert Bye of Penrhiwceiber with his Victoria Cross at Buckingham Palace, on 5th September, 1917

**78** Police Inspector John Clinch, senior officer of Mountain Ash Police 1930-34

**79** Police Sergeant Edgar George, the best known figure in Mountain Ash

**80**  Tom Fantham, now 84, from Penrhiwceiber, at the wheel of a 6½ litre Le Mans Bentley owned by
Sir Ronald Gunter of London. Tom spent his whole life with cars and buses

**81**  Field Marshall Sir Bernard Montgomery drives through Glyngwyn Street, Miskin, in 1946

**82** Gracie Fields holds Marion (Llewellyn) Jones in her arms at the Pavilion in February, 1938. Gracie sang to a packed house at a concert held in aid of the Boot and Shoe Fund

**83** One of the best known personalities in Mountain Ash, Arthur Hillier, at the door of one of his two hairdressing and sweet shops in Oxford Street

**84**  The Opening of Caedrawnant in 1951. Centre are Coun. and Mrs. W. M. Rees of Penrhiwceiber. On their left are Couns. Miss Mia George and Mrs. Lillian Watts

**85**  Coun. William Morgan and Mrs. Eunice Morgan enter Nazareth Church on Civic Sunday, 1964

**86** These five-foot leeks were fixed on the front of the "Dai Dower Special" train which went from Aberdare to London for the Jake Tuli Fight at Haringey Arena in 1958. Dower outpointed Tuli for the Commonwealth title. Coun. Dick Nelms, left, and Coun. Arthur Hillier display the leeks grown specially by Tom Hill

**87** Arthur Hayman of Lyle Street, nearing retirement in 1965 fondly cleans "Sal", the Council's steamroller which he nursed and drove for 43 years. Sal gave way to a modern diesel roller after Arthur's retirement

**88**   A happy occasion in Aberdare. Left to right: Helen Evans, daughter of Ioan Evans, M.P., (next to her), Mrs. Maria Evans, Disc-jockey Vince Saville, Mrs. Eunice Morgan, Coun. William Morgan (Mayor), and Ernest Arbery, Cancer Research Organiser

**89**   Well-known artist Vic Llewelyn of Cefn Pennar at his easel

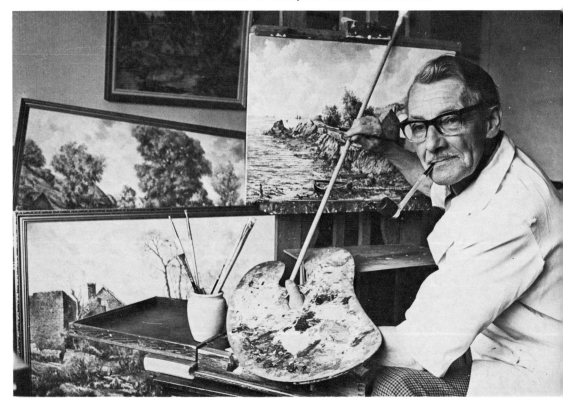

**90** Last of the old shoe-makers in Mountain Ash, Cliff Parfitt. He made shoes as well as repairing them

**91** Cliff Parfitt at his old Singer machine—a 1978 photograph

**93** Mrs. Sarah Jane Anstee of the Triangle, Mountain Ash, in 1978

**92** Mr. and Mrs. Dai Llewellyn, both in their eighties

**94** Mr. & Mrs. Emilio Piccaro, present owners of the Express Café, Oxford Street, formerly Charlie Fulgoni's Cadona Club

**95** Plaid Cymru members, left to right: Clayton Jones, County Coun. Pauline Jarman, and Member of Parliament Dafydd Wigley, at the Restoration Scheme Plant, Cwmcynon, Penrhiwceiber

# Trade and Collieries

**96** Ex-L.M.S. locomotive No. 48761—a 2.8.0, speeds into Mountain Ash, August, 1961

**97** Duffryn Colliery Locomotives, 1900

**98** The Taff Railway Station, Oxford Street, Mountain Ash, 1912

**99** Penrhiwceiber Railway Station, Taff Vale Railway

**100** Lipton's well-known shop in Oxford Street. Centre: Manager Mr. John Thomas, known as Thomas Lipton; on his right Miss Olwen Evans, sister of Mrs. Gladys Gardner of Fox Street. Date: 1919

**101** Richard-Hurt the fish and poultry dealers in Oxford Street, now Webber's wet-fish shop. On the left is the owner Mr. Richard Hurt with his daughter Joan in 1929

**102** Evans and Tucker's cake shop, Oxford Street. The firm had bakeries in Stream Street and Woodland Street. The young lady is Miss Lynne Tucker

**103** A trade card similar to those used by trades and professions in the early 1900s

**104** A "fat" pay packet for a coal miner in 1929

**105**  Glyngwyn Level, one of the proliferation of coal-extracting levels found in Mountain Ash at the beginning of the century

**106**  George Pit, Cefn Pennar, 1905

107   Nixon's Navigation Colliery, 1908

108   Lower Duffryn Colliery, Cwm Pennar, 1910

*Duffryn Deep Colliery, Mountain Ash*

**109**   Deep Duffryn Colliery, Caegarw in 1916

**110**   Penrikyber Colliery, Penrhiwceiber, 1917

**111** Cwmpennar Colliery, 1910

**112** Penrikyber Colliery, 1972

**113** Cwmcynon Colliery, Penrhiwceiber, 1926

**114** Victoria Street "Coons", 1926

# Carnivals

**115** Archie Lewis holds the rein of his horse Nancy who won so many carnival competitions in the 1930s. Bill Thomas is the man aboard

**116** Mountain Ash Highlander Charades Band, known as "The Jocks", in 1926. Centre right is Dai Llewellyn

**117** Darran Las "Chinks" band parade in Penrhiwceiber Road, 1926. In the front playing the big horn is Jack James (father of Mrs. Maisie Creech). Behind him is Fred James, Maisie's father, and to his left Maisie's cousin Wil James. The leader was Phil Jackson, step-father of Mrs. Thelma Bevan

**118** St. John's Church pantomime "Mother Goose", 1969

# Music and the Pavilion

119   The construction of the Pavilion in 1901

**120** The choirs are all set for the opening of the 1905 National Eisteddfod Concert in the Pavilion

**121** Members of the Penrhiwceiber and District Juvenile Choir, winner of the Chief Choral Competition for Children Under 16, August 1950, Caerffili

122   A 1935 picture of Penrikyber Colliery Male Choir, Penrhiwceiber

123     Mountain Ash "Glyndwr" Concert Male Choir. American Tour 1919-20.
Standing, left to right: J. O. Jones, M.E. (President), J. N. O. Williams, Rhys Thomas, Hy. Evans, D. Teifi Davies (Treasurer), Stephen Jenkins, Tom Davies (Secretary), Geo. Anthony, D. Pennar Williams, D. J. Davies, M.E. (President).
Sitting: M. J. Edwards, Sydney Charles, B. Davies (Chairman), T. Glyndwr Richards (Conductor), W. Evans, L.R.A.M. (Accompanist), Gomer David, Dd. Lewis

**124**  The Three Valleys Festival Committee of 1932.
Back row: C. C. D. Jones, J.P., D. J. Price, C. C. D. Thomas, Griff Davies, T. J. Thomas, F. O. Dyer.
Centre Row: R. C. Morgan (Chief Steward), Dan Edwards (conductor), P. Davies (conductor), W. J. Evans (conductor), W. J. Watkins (conductor), Sam Davies (Marshall), J. Lewis, C. W. Dixon (Asst. Sec.), D. T. Evans (Joint Sec.), Dr. A. T. Jones.
Seated: Rev. G. T. Gravell, Mrs. A. J. Jones, Mrs. R. W. Burgess, R. W. Burgess, W. A. Morgan (Chairman), Dr. Malcolm Sargent (conductor), Mrs. J. H. Bruce, Mrs. G. Davies, J. Charles McClean (Joint Sec.)

**125**  The Hibernian Band of Mountain Ash, conductor Danny Bryant, parade in Penrhiwceiber in 1953.
Dai Llewellyn plays the drum

126 Mountain Ash and District Choral Society at their first public appearance in January, 1966. They performed "Hiawatha's Wedding Feast"

128 Sir Malcolm Sargent takes the stage for t▐
Eist◄

**127** Penrhiwceiber Children's Choir at their highly successful tour of Germany in 1971

sed choirs on the last night of the 1946 National
vilion

# The Hunt

**129** A 1962 shot of the Ystrad Hunt outside the Jeffrey Arms (then the Jeffries Hotel) in Caegarw. Landlord Glyn Edwards and Ted Demery stand together near the left hand pillar

**130** Steam Ship "Adriatic", in which Mountain Ash's most famous choir, the T. Glyndwr Richards' choir, travelled to America where they sang before President and Mrs. Theodore Roosevelt at the White House

# Nos Galan
## 1958–73

**131** A happy shot at the graveside of Guto Nythbran in Llanwonno Churchyard on New Year's Eve, 1958—the occasion of the first ever Nos Galan. Left to right: Coun. Miss Mia George, Chairman Mr. Evan Lodwick, B.E.M., Council Clerk Mr. Raymond Richards, Mrs. A. Hillier, Mrs. B. Hewson, Brian Hewson, Stuart Jones, Coun. Arthur Hillier (Chairman of the Council), Coun. Dick Owen, Coun. Lyn Clark (behind), sprinter Peter Radford and Mrs. Morgan of the Brynffynnon

**132** Stan Eldon wins the first Nos Galan 4 miles in 1958. A massive crowd turned out that night

**133** Celebrations in the Town Hall after the 1960 races.
Standing, back: Norman Horrell, Bernard Baldwin, Derek Ibbotson, Coun. Miss Mia George, Gwilym Morgan and Ron Jones.
Front: Eddie Strong, John Merriman, Stan Eldon, 4 miles winner Martin Hyman, and Bruce Tulloh

**134** Oxford Street, 30th December, 1962—the night before Nos Galan. Organiser Bernard Baldwin shows his paces against the fastest white runner on earth at that time, the Polish sprinter Wieslaw Maniak, who two years earlier finished fourth in a blanket finish in the Olympic 100 metres final in Rome

**135** Coun. Sam Parfitt, Chairman of the Council, assisted by Coun. Miss Mia George, lights the Nos Galan beacon in front of the Town Hall, New Year's Eve, 1961

**136** Bruce Tulloh wins the 1961 Men's Mile in Penrhiwceiber in 4m. 31 secs.

**137** Start of the 1961 Nos Galan 4 miles, in Oxford Street. Winner Eddie Strong of Bristol A.C. clocked a new record time of 18m 40secs.

**138**  The Nos Galan Committee, 1960-61. Patron Lord Aberdare is seated centre. Standing behind Lord Aberdare on his right is Evan Lodwick, B.E.M., and on Lord Aberdare's left Jack Anthony-Bennett, Treasurer

**139**  1964 Mystery Runner Stan Eldon receives his trophy from Coun. William Morgan in the Council Chamber

**140**  1966 Mystery Runner Mary Rand lights the beacon at the Town Hall

**141** Ron Jones gets a good start in one of the heats of the 1965 Nos Galan 100 yards in Oxford Street. He went on to win the final in 9.8 seconds

**142** David Bedford, well on his way to victory in the 1969 midnight race, as he passes the bottom of Pryce Street with 2 miles to go

**143** Rita (Lincoln) Ridley wins the 1969 Women's Mile in Penrhiwceiber for the third time, in a new record time of 4m 54.7 secs.

**144** Julian Goater of St. Edmund Hall, Oxford University wins the 1972 Nos Galan 4 miles. Mrs. Irene Lisle and R.R.C. official Gordon Doubleday record his victory

**145** Coun. David Jenkins, Mayor of Cynon Valley greets the 1984 Mystery Runners at the Town Hall. Holding the torch is Mystery Runner 'Present', Steve Jones, with 'Future' Lisa Hopkins and 'Past' David Bedford

# Nos Galan 1984

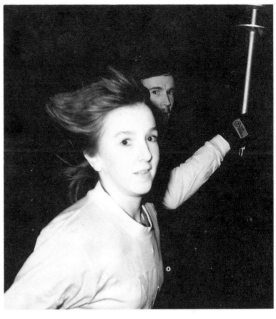

**146** James Hill of Newport Harriers breasts the tape to win the 1984 Midnight Mile race in 4m. 10 secs.

**147** Diminutive Lisa Hopkins of Mountain Ash, Mystery Runner of the Future, 1984, shares the carrying of the torch with Steve Jones

**148** A joyful welcome for the Mystery Runners at Perthcelyn in 1984. Mrs. Gwen Owen holds the torch while Steve Jones, winner of the Chicago marathon in world record time, signs an autograph

# Sport

**149** Three of the greatest fighters of all time, who all fought in Mountain Ash. Left to right: Freddy Welsh, Tom Thomas and Jim Driscoll. Their Lonsdale Belts were awarded for three successful British Championship fights at any one weight

**150** Tommy Farr, here seen in action at the Market Hall, Abergavenny, fought several times in the Pavilion. Farr became British and Empire Heavyweight champion in 1937

**151** Mountain Ash Rugby Football Club, 1892/93
Dr. E. P. Evans, J.P., W. Beynon, T. Parrott, A. Allen, D. S. Lewis, J. Phillips, K. Mills, W. Eynon,
H. Hale (Secretary), J. Murphy, T. Bishop, J. Sullivan, B. Tiley (Captain), J. Hoskins, J. Carey, F. Mears,
S. C. Lewis, J. H. Eynon, D. J. Thomas, W. Bradford, W. Phillips

**152** Mountain Ash R.F.C., 1901/2
J. Grant (Trainer), H. Hughes, J. Muxworthy, A. Price, S. Muxworthy, W. T. Osborne, A. Fryer, G. Mears,
J. Deere, H. Hale (Secretary), T. Perrott, D. Fryer, R. Carpenter, M. Price, T. Walton, A. W. Jones, L. Deere,
Geo. Edwards

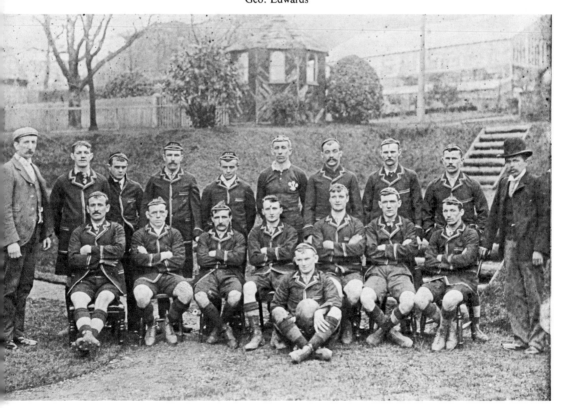

**153** Penrhiwceiber Soccer Team, 1926

**154** Caegarw Junior School soccer team, 1948. Headmaster Ben Thomas on left and Games Master Nev. Lukey-Davies on right

**155** Mountain Ash Y.M.C.A. Basketball team, 1953-54.
Back, left to right: Brian Evans, David Bradwick, John Webber, Billy Jones.
Front: John Price, Noel Evans, John Hiscox, Brian Roberts, Ceri Evans

**156** Mountain Ash Y.M.C.A. Under 18s Basketball Team, who won the 1958 Welsh Y.M.C.A. Championship.
Back, left to right: Roy Bird, Wayne Stephens.
Front: John Price, Henry Shanahan, David Thomas

157  Mountain Ash A.T.C. Soccer team, 1950, winners of the Welsh A.T.C. cup that year. Left to right, standing: Flt. Lt. Isaac Watts, P. James, G. Brown, D. Davies, R. Brown, B. Stokes, D. Lewis, J. Lewis. Seated: D. Vaughan, G. Jones, G. Lewis, D. Bevan, R. Evans

158  Caegarw Secondary School Soccer team, 1952/53, winners of the Cynon Star Shield that year. Back, left to right: Ronnie James, Terry Llewellyn, Des Edwards, Ray Evans, Frank Hole, Gwynfor Richards, Brian Eggleton and "Curly". Seated: Mr. Henry Luther-Davies, Headmaster, Peter Evans, Beyham Williams (capt.), Brian Davies, and form teacher Mr. N. Lukey-Davies.

159   Caegarw ex-schoolboys rugby team, 1924/25

**160**   Benny Williams, captain of Everton and Wales, season 1933/34, at Glasbrook Field, Penrhiwceiber

**161**   A 1951 shot of Bill Perkins the International quoits player, here seen beating Scots champion John Kilpatrick 21 points to 9, in the international that year at Annan, Scotland

**162**  Newtown Quoits team and officials, 1932.
Top row, left to right: G. Hawkins, J. Olden, T. Bush, G. Mears, A. Hooper, A. Duden, W. Collins, W. Watts.
Middle row: M. Ruck, W. Vokins, W. Bray, W. Mellish, S. Bishop, B. Mears, L. Beer, W. Perkins, O. Stevens,
W. Bray (Club Sec.).
Bottom row: M. Thomas, J. Christopher, Dr. A. Jones, W. Jones (capt.), W. Morgan, T. Roderick, S. Griffiths

**163**  Pakistan Eaglets Cricket Team, on a tour of this country, played Mountain Ash in August, 1953.
Coun. Miss Mia George congratulates skipper Mahmood on his fine innings of 69. Also in the picture are
Steve Griffiths, B.E.M., J.P., chairman of the local cricket club, and Mountain Ash captain I. Harvey